MINKE
WHALES

D1406517

Printed in China

00 01 02 03 04 5 4 3 2 1

Library of Congress Cataloging-in-Publication Data
Hoelzel, Rus.
Minke Whales / Rus Hoelzel and Jonathan Stern
p. cm. -- (WorldLife library)
Summary: Discusses the biology and behavior of the minke whale and the relationship between these creatures and humans.
Includes bibliographical references.
ISBN 0-89658-490-9 (alk. paper)
1. Minke whale–Juvenile literature. [1. Minke Whales. 2. Whales-] 1. Stern, Jonathan.
II. Title. III. World life library.
QL737.C424 H63 2000
599.5'24–dc21   99-089957
CIP

Distributed in Canada by Raincoast Books, 8680 Cambie Street, Vancouver, B.C. V6P 6M9

Published by Voyageur Press, Inc.
123 North Second Street, P. O. Box 338, Stillwater, MN 55082, U.S.A.
651-430-2210, fax 651-430-2211

Educators, fundraisers, premium and gift buyers, publicists and marketing managers: Looking for creative products and new sales ideas? Voyageur Press books are available at special discounts when purchased in quantities, and special editions can be created to your specifications. For details contact the marketing department at 800-888-9653.

Photographs copyright © 2000 by

Front cover © Mark Carwardine (Still Pictures)
Back cover © Joel Bennett (Oxford Scientific Films)
Page 1 © Bill Wood (Bruce Coleman)
Page 3 © PGH Evans / SWF
Page 4 © C Swann
Page 6 © Douglas David Seifert
Page 9 © Michael W Newcomer
Page 10 © H Sato
Page 13 © PGH Evans / SWF
Page 14 © Kelvin Aitken (NHPA)
Page 17 © C Swann
Page 19 © C Swann
Page 20 © Francisco J Erize (Bruce Coleman)
Page 23 © Kelvin Aitken (NHPA)
Page 24 © Michael W Newcomer
Page 26 © Jason Gedamke

Page 27 © Jonathan Stern
Page 29 © H Sato
Page 30 © Ben Osborne (Oxford Scientific Films)
Page 32 © Richard Fairbairns
Page 33 © H Sato
Page 34 © Michael W Newcomer
Page 35 © P Stevick
Page 36 © PGH Evans / SWF
Page 38 © Jonathan Stern
Page 39 © C Swann
Page 40 © C Swann
Page 41 © Robert Nordblom (Marine Mammal Images)
Page 43 © C Swann
Page 46 © Michael W Newcomer
Page 48 © Michael W Newcomer

MINKE
WHALES

A. Rus Hoelzel & S. Jonathan Stern

WORLDLIFE
LIBRARY

Voyageur Press

Contents

Minke Whales

The first scientific description of the minke whale was by Fabricus in 1780 and was followed by their taxonomic classification as *Balaenoptera acutorostrata* in 1804 by Lacépède. However, minke whales had been familiar to coastal-dwelling peoples in temperate and sub-polar waters for a long time prior to that. While frequently seen in the open ocean, minke whales also inhabit bays and fiords looking for food, and can often be seen from shore. They feature in local traditions and myths, and were to some cultures a source of food. Inhabitants of coastal North Atlantic regions have hunted minke whales on a small scale for centuries. Native Americans living on Cape Flattery of what is now Washington State occasionally killed minke whales, but focussed more on gray and humpback whales. The minke featured in some of the myths and iconography of Native Americans in the Pacific Northwest, although relatively infrequently compared to the killer whale. While some of their habits were known, as with many cetacean species, it was not until commercial whaling began targeting minke whales that we began to learn in some detail about their natural history.

The minke whale is the smallest of the so-called 'finner' whales, which includes blue, fin, sei and Bryde's whales. In fact it is the second smallest of all baleen whales; only the pygmy right whale is smaller. Finner whales are so named because, unlike other baleen whale species, they have a falcate (sickle-shaped) fin on their backs known as the dorsal fin. They are all sleek, torpedo-shaped whales, capable of swimming at high speeds. The common name, minke, is a reference to a Norwegian whaler, Meincke, who thought the minke whales he saw were actually its much larger cousins, blue whales. A typical fisherman's story! Minke whales are found worldwide in temperate and polar waters in both the northern and southern hemispheres.

As with all baleen whales, female minke whales are, on average, a bit bigger than males and produce one calf after a gestation period of about 10 to 11 months, with a four to six month lactation period. This is a relatively short gestation period for a baleen whale, and the females are thought to be able to produce a calf every year.

Three different forms of minke whales have been described (and a recent re-classification has proposed two distinct species: see 'Evolution and Regional Differences' for more detail). The form in the North Atlantic and Pacific oceans (*B. acutorostrata*) has white baleen plates and a white patch on the middle third of the pectoral fin. The 'dwarf' minke is restricted to the southern ocean, and has white from the middle of the pectoral fin extending onto the shoulder. The more numerous southern form (proposed new species: *B. bonaerensis*) has white baleen in the front of its mouth, darker baleen in the rear, and usually lacks any white on the pectoral fin. We will discuss the genetics and management implications of these differences in later chapters.

In the North Atlantic there are an estimated 149,000 minke whales (the likely range is 120,000–182,000). In the western North Pacific and Sea of Okhotsk, there are an estimated 25,000 (a range of 12,800–48,600) and there are about 22,000 in the Sea of Japan and the Yellow Sea. There are an unknown number of minke whales in the rest of the North Pacific, though a population size of 631 has been estimated off California, Oregon and Washington, and this is considered separate from a migratory stock in Alaska. The largest population by far is in the Antarctic where there are an estimated 761,000 minke whales (a range of 510,000–1,400,000). An unknown number of 'dwarf' minke whales are restricted to the southern oceans.

Our understanding of minke whales, and other whales as well, to a large extent parallels the development of commercial whaling (see page 37). However, since the early 1980s, studies using benign research techniques have provided an insight into the population structure, ecology and behavior of minke whales. Most of this book will focus on the results of those studies.

Food and Feeding

One afternoon we sat in our 16-ft (5-m) skiff in mirror-calm waters off the San Juan Islands, Washington State, waiting for the minke whale we called Jackie (named after Jackie Onassis; it was our most photographed whale). The whale had been underwater for over five minutes, and after this long it was not uncommon for us to lose sight of it. We also had little idea of where to expect the next surfacing, so we stood with the engine off, scanning the horizon and listening. On such calm water we could hear the whale at some distance, often before we could see it. After five to ten minutes without a sighting we were listening hard. On this day, as we stood there in near silence, an enormous eruption of water, whale and scattering fish broke the surface not 33 ft (10 m) from the boat. While one of us scrambled for the camera and the other to start the engine, the minke whale surfaced a few more times and then returned to deeper water for another five minutes or so. This is one of the ways minke whales in this part of the world feed on herring.

The minke whale is a rorqual, which means 'red whale' in Norwegian. The rorquals include all the finners and the humpback whale (all the Balaenopterid whales). Each has a long series of grooves in its throat, and when they feed they fill this expandable cavity with prey and volumes of water. Their bloated throats expose the pink skin within the grooves, (hence the name, rorqual) and dramatically alter their shape. From above, a feeding fin or blue whale looks very much like a giant tadpole. The minke, breaching with a full throat, looks like a serious beer guzzler with a small, pointy head. Their baleen is relatively short and well adapted for larger prey, such as fish, although they also feed on large crustaceans, such as krill (their main prey in the Antarctic).

Minkes in the eastern North Pacific feed on fish as individual specialists.

Minke whale 'breach-feeding' in Nemuro Strait, Japan, showing its distended throat.

Some take their prey in pre-packaged parcels, concentrated at the surface by feeding seabirds. Others (Jackie for example) do the work themselves, herding fish up from below, trapping them against the air-water interface. The fish boil at the surface in a hopeless attempt to escape into the air and are engulfed by the gaping jaws of the minke whale in full breach.

We were able to learn about the behavior of individual specialists because we could identify individuals from their photographs. To do this we needed full-frame photographs from a position parallel to the whale, and from both sides. We used 300 mm lenses and very fast film so that we could photograph the moving whale, in focus, from a rocking boat. We relied primarily on three characteristics. The first is the dorsal fin, which is approximately 1 ft (30 cm) tall and located two-thirds of the way back along the dorsal surface. The fin can be a variety of shapes from hooked to triangular, nicked or notched in various places, and darkly or lightly pigmented. While this is a very useful characteristic, it is not always enough on its own to identify an individual whale. The second feature is a swathe of pale pigmentation on the front flank called the chevron, usually seen in three parts. This pattern of pigmentation varied between individuals, but was relatively difficult to photograph. Finally, we used round or oval white scars, 1–2 in (25–50 mm) across, the cause of which we still don't know for sure. The position of these white marks on the flank was very useful, but needed to be updated each year as new scars were acquired and old scars faded. Once we established a photo-ID of an individual whale, we could usually identify it from less than perfect photographs (more distant and angular shots, as were sometimes necessary).

Individually known whales from our study could be categorized into two broad types of foraging specialists, which we referred to as 'breach-feeders' and 'bird-ball feeders'. Each type was seen in particular locations around the islands, apparently where the conditions best suited that foraging strategy. The breach-feeders were seen most often in deep bays between islands. They

*Only half of the flukes are visible on this whale which has just lunged
through a flock of feeding seabirds, and consumed their prey right out from under
them. The birds explode into the air just before the minke lunges.*

This is the 'dwarf-form' minke whale. Note the extensive white pigmentation on the pectoral flipper, extending up onto the body. This is distinct from the northern form, which has a white band restricted to the center of the fin, and the southern form which usually has no white band at all.

would surface for a relatively extended period of five to eight blows, followed by a long dive. At the end of the long dive they sometimes resurfaced in a vertical breach with a mouthful of fish, hence the name.

The bird-ball feeders were most often seen over shallow banks, although sometimes they were seen in the same bays as the breach-feeders. These whales seemed to patrol back and forth over the banks, surfacing for a shorter series of breaths, followed by relatively short dives. At the same time, gulls would flock to concentrations of prey at the surface; the fish kept there by diving birds (such as murres, auklets and puffins) feeding below the surface. The minke whale would come upon these dense schools of fish at the surface, and as the birds exploded into the air, consume the fish in a fast, shallow lunge. By this strategy, the whale seems to expend relatively little effort, but feeds less frequently than whales that feed by the apparently more energetically demanding breach-feeding strategy. Our hypothesis was that this balance, together with the need for individuals to learn where and how to feed by each strategy, may explain why over the years we saw most individuals specializing on one strategy or the other. Out of 23 whales, 20 were seen feeding by only one method, while three were 'switch-hitters'. The strategy of feeding on prey concentrated by birds is also known to occur with minkes in other parts of the world, such as among the Hebrides in Scotland.

In waters near Monterey Bay, California, surface-feeding behaviors were only rarely observed. Here, whales move along the coast in a more or less linear fashion, within the 50 fathom (90 m) contour. One very calm day, we followed a whale as it traveled along in a fairly predictable fashion, surfacing four times every seven minutes. At one point the whale appeared just below the boat, on its side, mouth open wide, engulfing a school of fish, only to surface seven minutes after the previous surfacing, and continue on its predictable way. This underscores the fact that surface behaviors only tell us part of the story, since whales spend more than 90 per cent of their time underwater, out of sight.

The idealized life-history strategy of baleen whales includes a summer of intense feeding in high-latitude waters. During this time, energy in the form of blubber is stored and is the primary energy source during long migrations, and while on lower latitude breeding and calving grounds in winter. However it is clear that deviations from this strategy are common for finner whales, and this is especially true of the minke whale. Among the finners, minkes have the lowest blubber to body weight ratio, and therefore may not have as much relative storage capacity. This could mean that they would need a prolonged feeding season, or to spend less time and energy on migration.

Studies of their energy requirements and intake rates suggest that all finners may need to feed year-round, although some more than others, and perhaps all at a reduced level in winter. In almost every location where minke whales feed in summer, they are also occasionally observed in winter. This is true even at the Antarctic ice edge where krill, their primary prey in the area, overwinter. Fin whales have been seen in bays of Kodiak Island, Alaska, feeding on herring in winter, and recent observations even confirm blue whales feeding in winter off Baja, California. If individuals didn't migrate, thermal stress would not necessarily differ significantly from summer to winter, as in some places water temperature can be warmer in winter than in summer. While there is much known about these species, there is much we still don't know about the migratory and reproductive behavior of the finner whales. In most cases, we still do not know the location of breeding grounds, or the extent to which the feeding and fasting concept applies to finner whales in all parts of the world.

Studies based especially on data from whaling confirm that minkes do feed more in the summer than in the winter, even if the difference is sometimes small compared to other baleen whales. They also provide details on the variety of prey species taken. We observed feeding on herring fry and sandlance in the eastern North Pacific, although we couldn't determine the full

range of prey that may have been taken there. Minkes in the western North Pacific were found to have fed on seven species of fish, three species of euphausiids (a shrimp-like crustacean), and one species of copepod. In that study, the most important prey species was the Pacific saury, a fish that accounted for 80 per cent of their diet, and a related study indicated that most feeding occurred during the day. Another study describes some North Pacific minkes preying exclusively on euphausiids, some exclusively on fish, with the difference correlated to location and time of year. In the Okhotsk Sea, most whales preyed on herring, while in Salkhalin most preyed on pollock. Studies spanning 40 years also suggested a shift in prey choice over time. In the eastern North Atlantic, minkes fed on 12 species of fish, although again there were dominant species in the diet in different places and at different times. For example, in the north near Spitsbergen and Bear Island, capelin was preferred, while further south off Norway and Russia herring was the most important prey.

In the Antarctic the main prey of minke whales is krill (e.g. *Euphausia superba*), as for most baleen whales feeding there. This shrimp-like animal is a key element of the Antarctic ecosystem, and a tremendously abundant food resource for many marine mammal, fish, cephalopod and seabird species. It has been estimated that an 'average' minke whale consumes about 970 lb (440 kg) of krill per day during its three to four month stay in the Antarctic, and that the total population of minke whales in the Antarctic consumes approximately 35 million tonnes of krill annually. Minke whales digest krill, especially the wax ester that makes up a large part of the krill body mass, with an efficiency of 93 per cent compared to 84 per cent for crabeater seals, which are themselves very efficient compared to many other species. It is thought that the main difference is in the multi-chambered stomach system of the minke whale (compared to the seal's single stomach), and the symbiotic bacteria within it. This digestive system also gives minke whales a high efficiency at digesting herring and other fish.

Evolution and Regional Differences

The three main groups of baleen whales (the gray whale, right whales and the rorquals) probably diverged over the last 5–20 million years. There is just one extant species of gray whale, a bottom-feeding whale with short, coarse baleen. The right whales are large and buoyant, with very long baleen suited to the task of sieving tiny plankton in dense concentrations. All rorqual species have intermediate baleen adapted to taking relatively larger prey, such as krill and small fish. However the main distinction is their accordion-like expanding throats. All rorquals are fast and sleek, and fill a niche quite distinct from the other types of baleen whale. One of these, the humpback, has some unique adaptations. The others are the so-called finner whales, which include the minke.

All of the 'finner' whales share the same general form, but differ especially in color and overall size. The minke is the smallest at about 26 to 33 ft (8 to 10 m) long, Bryde's whales are about 46 ft (14 m), sei whales about 60 ft (18 m), fin whales about 82 ft (25 m), and the blue whale can grow to over 98 ft (30 m). There are also subtle aspects of body shape and form that distinguish each species. For the blue, Bryde's and minke there also exists a 'dwarf' form, which tends to be very similar to the 'ordinary' form in morphology, but grows to a smaller overall size. The smaller blue whale, (reaching to 70–80 ft (21–24 m) in length), is recognized as a subspecies, and called the 'pygmy blue whale'. It shares much of the same geographic range as the larger form, although it is most common in the Indian Ocean. The dwarf Bryde's whale was recognized only recently, and is found in a population near the Solomon Islands. A study, using genetic markers, of this form showed that the small form had diverged from the Bryde's whale at about the same time as the other Balaenopterid species were diverging. In other words, it looked to be a previously unrecognized species of baleen whale!

The minke dwarf form is found in waters off South Africa, Australia, and in the Indian Ocean. It is similar in coloration to minke whales seen in the northern hemisphere, although the white on its pectoral flippers is more extensive. This is an interesting distinction; minke whales found in the southern oceans usually have no white on their pectoral flippers. The northern and southern forms have long been recognized as different subspecies. Genetic studies confirm the distinction, and even suggest a likely species-level difference between the southern and northern forms. A recent classification of cetaceans proposes separating these two forms into different species, B. *acutorostrata* in the northern hemisphere and B. *bonaerensis* in the southern hemisphere. Interestingly, the dwarf form, which is found in the same waters as the southern form (B. *bonaerensis*), is actually more closely related to the northern form (B. *acutorostrata*).

In general, minke whales show geographic differentiation which suggests that they tend to stay relatively close to where they were born when they mate. This partitioning of genetic information within a species is typical, though among the baleen whales, the minke whale stands out. At the broadest geographic level, there is differentiation between the two hemispheres that is much more pronounced than it is for other finner whales. Even at the local level, minkes seem more likely to be differentiated genetically from nearby populations than at least some other species in this genus. For example, the population along the east coast of Japan is differentiated from a population just 600 miles (965 km) away along the coast of Korea. These two populations migrate north in summer to feeding grounds in the Okhotsk Sea, and although they mix there, they tend to return to their natal populations to breed. In other parts of the world we know less about the evolution of population differences in minke whales. In the North Atlantic there are two genetic lineages found on feeding grounds, but we don't yet know if this indicates distinct breeding populations. The kind of site fidelity we see in the San Juan Islands (see pages 31–35) is consistent with the pattern of isolated populations seen elsewhere in the North Pacific.

*A dwarf-form minke whale photographed off the Great Barrier Reef, Australia.
Note the 'chevrons' of pale pigmentation on the back. These are often
useful in the identification of individual whales.*

A Solitary Life

When following a minke whale in our study areas, we were often able to stay with it for hours. On some occasions we were with the same whale all day. Most of the time they would apparently either be feeding or traveling, and in Washington and British Columbia, we could distinguish these behaviors as follows. Feeding behavior (which is described in more detail on pp 11–19) was characterized by relatively erratic behavior at the surface, punctuated by breaching or lunging and often by the visible scattering of fish into the air. Traveling was characterized by a regular pattern of breathing and a relatively consistent direction of movement. We often observed minke whales traveling between places where they would then stop and feed. Some of these feeding areas would attract a number of minke whales, and we'd have trouble keeping track of who was who. However, as they each pursued prey or traveled between feeding sites, they rarely appeared to do so in a co-ordinated way, as for example killer whales do. Most of the time they seemed to be quite independent of one another.

Social species, like killer whales and many other dolphins, travel in a coherent way. Individuals may be separated by some distance, but when they change directions or behavior, they all tend to do so together. On occasion minke whales in our study areas would do something like this, but it didn't happen very often, and it didn't last very long. On these occasions we would see two or three whales traveling side by side, within 15–80 ft (5–25 m) of each other, surfacing at the same time, and moving in the same direction. This would last at most for a few surfacings, but for that short time their movements did seem to be co-ordinated. We have no idea what they were doing when this occurred.

Pairs and trios of minke whales have also been seen elsewhere, but it is more common for single animals to be seen. Concentrations of minkes on

A pair of dwarf minke whales in synchronous behavior.
This type of co-ordinated behavior has been seen in most populations
of minke whales, although it is much more common to see
individuals on their own in most locations.

their feeding grounds are apparently proportional to the abundance of the resources available. In polar waters where prey is very abundant, groups of up to several hundred have been seen. In the Antarctic the clustering of minke whales was investigated on three major feeding grounds. Schools of minke whales within larger aggregations were randomly distributed, and the mean number of whales within a school increased with the density of an aggregation. Clustering was greater within bays than it was in open water.

Dwarf minke whales are seen for a few months within the relatively protected waters of the lee of the Great Barrier Reef in the Austral winter. Here dozens of individuals may congregate around boats at anchor, sometimes for hours. It is not clear whether these congregations are the result of attraction to the boat, or represent one or more cohesive groups of interacting individuals that are passing by

The chevron pigmentation patterns as seen from the surface.

chance. Neither is it clear what dwarf minke whales are doing off the Great Barrier Reef. It may be a breeding ground (since some cow/calf pair sightings have been reported) or just a point along the migration between calving/breeding and feeding grounds.

A solitary lifestyle naturally raises the question of how minke whales find one another in order to mate. Very little is known about this. It is assumed that there are geographic regions where minke whales tend to go to breed, but few have been clearly identified. We had assumed that the whales in our study area were all adults, and that although some individuals had been seen throughout the year, for the most part mating and parturition took place elsewhere. Rarely we would see a pair of whales, one seemingly rather bigger than the other. And similar reports would come in to a whale sighting 'hotline'. We sometimes dismissed this as some sort of optical illusion (which could easily happen unless both whales surfaced at the same time, near each other, and going in the same direction). Eventually a very small minke whale, apparently a calf that had still been nursing, stranded on San Juan Island, and we were at last convinced that there was something to these 'small' minke sightings. All the same, even our apparently resident minke whales must have been doing most of their reproducing elsewhere.

This question of finding mates is common to all of the so-called finner species, none of which seem to have clearly defined breeding grounds (unlike humpback, gray and right whales). One suggestion is that they use acoustical signals to find one another. Each of these species produces very loud, low-frequency, repetitious sounds. Prior to noise pollution, for example from boats and drilling, these intense long-wavelength sounds might have been heard across ocean basins. They could have traversed the ocean in cold, deep-water channels, ideally suited to the transmission of low-frequency sound. Not much is known about minke whale vocalizations, but Minkes don't seem to produce quite as intense or low-frequency sounds as some of the larger finner whales, and so may not have the capacity to communicate over as great a distance. We spent a fair amount of time listening to minkes as they fed and traveled in the San Juans, and never heard a sound we could attribute to the minke whale. On the other hand, in other regions, especially at lower latitudes, minke whales vocalize relatively frequently. Most often they either produce low-frequency grunts and growls, or a rather more interesting train of thumping sounds. It has been suggested that the latter may be unique to each individual – a kind of 'signature' call, although more data is needed to know for sure.

Movement and Migration

To help trace a whale's movements over time, whalers have used numbered tags fired into the dorsal musculature of a whale (called Discovery tags). If a tagged individual was later killed during whaling, the date and location were compared with the date and location of tagging. While this technique provided evidence of seasonal movement for a number of whale species, for minke whales tag recoveries were rare. Only two whales marked in the Antarctic and later killed off Brazil provide direct evidence of migration. Beyond this, evidence for migrations comes from genetic markers and from seasonal shifts in abundance on feeding grounds, putative migration routes and breeding grounds.

Using photographs to identify individual whales has made it much easier to study their movements, especially for those species that can be easily identified in this way. For example, the underside of humpback whale flukes provides an individual mark almost like a fingerprint, and this has permitted the tracking of individuals over thousands of miles. Individual minkes can also be recognized from photos, but because this technique is based on less informative characteristics, and long-distance tracking of a large number of minkes by this technique will be more difficult, genetic 'tagging' would probably work better for this species. However, relatively small numbers of individual minkes have been identified photographically and kept track of for years in the North Pacific and North Atlantic. Some of these whales have been seen in the same areas over very long periods of time. The longest includes records of known minkes in the San Juan Islands first seen in 1980, and most recently seen in 1999. Some individuals stay in, or regularly return to, local near-shore regions year after year. Others may travel much greater distances, visit an area infrequently, or live further out to sea.

Photo-ID also helps assess the size of a population (e.g. through keeping track of the rate and location of re-sightings, a so-called 'mark and recapture' method). After success in the San Juan Islands, we began work off central California in 1984. We heard of reports that the area supported many individual minke whales. Most of the reports were from people based at a land station south of Monterey. However, when we identified and followed individual whales from that area, we found that the same few whales moved along shore, up the coast, then back down the coast, being sighted from shore over and over again.

The study area off Monterey was effectively bisected by deep water at the Carmel Submarine Canyon. Whales from the north would stop as they approached the canyon and head back north, while whales from the south would reverse course and head back south. In both cases, the minke whales seemed to prefer waters of less than 50 fathoms deep. Sometimes the canyon was frequented by feeding blue and humpback whales, but minke whales avoided these congregations and instead swam back and forth along the coast, often at the edge of kelp beds.

Northern minke whale surfacing off the Hebrides in Scotland.

Why do large, mobile animals such as minke whales tend to congregate in certain areas? The short answer is probably that while local resources vary over time, certain localities reliably offer the needed resource (although that can change). The suitability of a local site for feeding will depend on its productivity, but also on the adaptations of the predator, and on any learned specializations of individual animals. Productivity can vary within and between seasons, so there is also a temporal component to the identification of a good resource. In fact,

A number of round scars useful for individual
identification are visible on the back of this whale. It is not
known for certain what causes these scars, although some are
likely to be wounds inflicted by the cookiecutter shark.

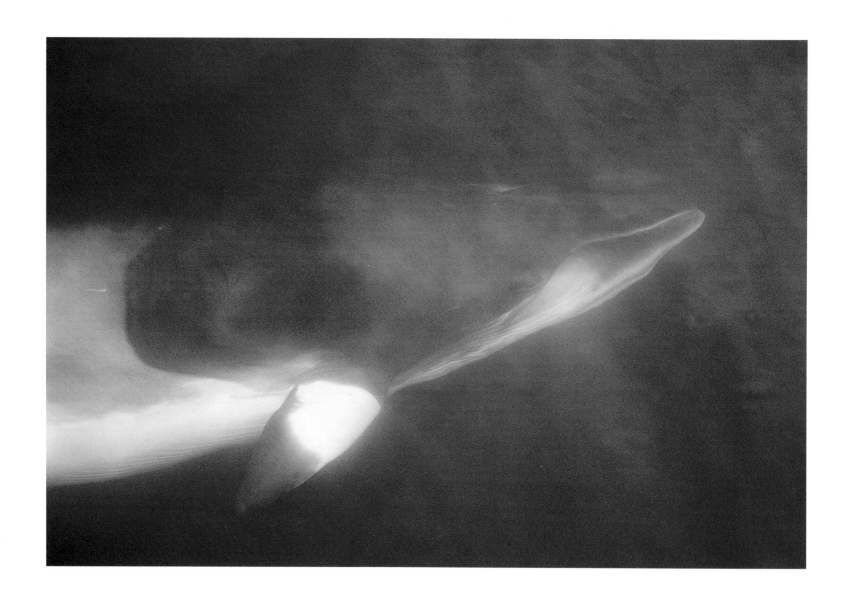

Northern minke whale just below the surface. The gular grooves common to all rorquals are visible, and
note the white pigmentation on the pectoral flipper. This band is restricted to the middle of the flipper in contrast
to the much more extensive white pigmentation seen on the flippers of the dwarf minke whale.

fine-scale variation in production can occur weekly, daily, or even from one hour to the next. Therefore, a whale may visit one of these areas or 'patches', and find food plentiful, or so scarce that it needs to move on and look for a better patch.

The rationale for seasonally returning to specific feeding grounds (or staying there year-round) is that they offer a more or less predictable source of food, even if the whale needs to scout around a bit looking for food while it's there. We watched minkes in the San Juans visiting and moving between feeding areas.

While within a patch they moved in a more or less random fashion, searching for prey. The areas between patches represent an 'energy sink', where more energy is being expended than taken in by the whale. So you'd expect them to waste little time moving between patches, and to choose an adjacent patch to move to when foraging at the current patch was unproductive. In the San Juans, this is just what they seemed to do.

A porpoising minke whale traveling fast.

Climate change (such as the current global warming) may affect the spatial distribution of some kinds of patches, or some of the physical processes that determine the productivity of the patch. If the pattern or extent of productivity is changed, the whales may need to spend more or less time searching for productive patches. This could have a variety of effects, including an effect on the feeding season or on the foraging range. This in turn could change the overall patterns of movement and population dynamics, and may well have occurred in the past as climate has changed over the millennia.

Minkes and Humans

The minke whale is familiar to coastal peoples in temperate regions around the world. Although often overlooked, on a calm day and given some patience, one can sometimes watch a minke from shore for hours. However, during that time, they may not do much more than surface in a series of three to five blows, followed by a dive of three to seven minutes. For this reason, in parts of the world where there are humpback whales, right whales, gray whales or killer whales, modern whale-watching tends to focus on those species. That isn't to say that whale-watchers don't ever stop to look at minkes, but that the more predictable 'show-whales' tend to be the feature. However, this isn't true everywhere: in Iceland and in the Hebrides in Scotland, whale-watchers enjoy minke-watching as the main event. Minke whales are relatively abundant in these areas, and whale-watch boats have good success at finding and staying near them. Minkes seem to be naturally curious, and will often approach a boat for a look, and may even bow-ride. In the Hebrides and off the Great Barrier Reef they sometimes approach and remain with a boat for hours, gently rolling and hovering just below the surface. On several occasions we have had minke whales at the bow of our boat off Washington State and California for an hour or more, alternating sides and rolling ventral-side-up with each pass by the bow, or swimming alongside just a few feet away.

The minke whale also holds the distinction of being the only baleen whale kept in captivity for the purpose of public display, though this didn't last long, as it soon broke out of its net enclosure. Of course, our dominant interaction with this species has been less benign. Though hunted locally by native cultures for hundreds of years, commercial whaling for minke whales was developed first in the North Atlantic by Iceland in 1914, and had increased significantly by the 1930s. Local coastal whaling operations that took minkes could be found in eastern Canada, Greenland, Iceland, Norway, Korea, China, Japan, Brazil, and

South Africa. In the Southern Ocean, large-scale commercial catches began in the early 1970s following the reduction of stocks of the larger whales, and by 1979 minkes were the only species taken by pelagic Antarctic whaling fleets. Many thousands were taken during this time, and used in a wide variety of products from cosmetics to mink food, as well as for human consumption. This continued until 1986 when a moratorium on commercial whaling came into effect. Prior to 1970, minkes were not considered an economically worthwhile quarry for pelagic whaling, as they are fast, hard to catch, and relatively small.

Close-up of minke lips.

Minke whales are currently hunted in the North Atlantic, Northwest Pacific and the Antarctic Ocean, primarily for human consumption. The quota for the Norwegian catch in 1999 was 753 whales, although only 589 were taken. This hunt is being undertaken without the approval of the International Whaling Commission (IWC). Hunts based from Japan are presently done under 'scientific' permit (also without IWC sanction). Current population estimates of 149,000 in the North Atlantic, 25,000 in the Northwest Pacific and 761,000 in the Antarctic have encouraged some to push for a resumption of whaling for minkes, and an assessment of the management implications is a stated objective of the Japanese scientific catch (which numbered over 500 in 1999). However, there are several unknowns and potential risks.

In the Northern hemisphere minke whales are taken in small-scale, shore-

Whale watchers enjoy a 'friendly' minke whale in near-shore waters off the Hebrides. Often a minke will hover nearby the boat, at or just under the surface, for hours at a time. Sometimes you might wonder just who's watching whom!

based operations and a single population is assumed to migrate past an area of localized whaling activities. In the southern hemisphere, large factory ships with several catcher boats are used to hunt in different areas where different stocks are thought to occur. However, data from the Northeast Pacific shows that coastal minke whales form relatively small, isolated breeding populations. A mixture of these populations has been specifically shown to pass along the migration routes during certain times of the year, and to mix on feeding grounds. Since the whales are hunted on their feeding grounds, and can't be distinguished visually, there is the risk that one population may be depleted more than another. Further, if one population is low in diversity for whatever reason, management strategy would be to preserve what variation is left. However, if the whales are all together in the same place while being hunted, avoiding the further depletion of a specific population will be quite difficult.

Minke entangled in rope and floats, probably from a fishing net.

There are two sides to conservation and management issues as they apply to whaling. The first is the practical question about how to manage a hunt so that the population doesn't decline and biodiversity is maintained, while remaining an economically viable endeavor for the whalers. On the other hand is the question of whether a species should be harvested at all, which is an ethical consideration. While there are many who have a firm view on the second question, the first can be very difficult to determine. It is not simply a question of taking a small proportion of a population. Information on spatial and temporal factors is also essential to a realistic estimate of the impact of a hunt. Other problems arise from the fact that these are naturally dynamic populations that are integrated into the relevant ecosystems as a whole. An increase in the population numbers of a competitor could reduce prey resources and add pressure to a hunted stock.

This type of argument has also been made in defence of whaling. For example, it has been suggested that the relatively numerous minke whales in the southern hemisphere are out-competing the endangered blue whale for krill, and thereby keeping blue whale population numbers low. Hunting more minkes, so the argument goes, could free up prey for the blue whales. However, there are a number of key assumptions that may or may not hold. The argument assumes that krill abundance is limiting and that the two species overlap at the relevant time and space. It also assumes that freed resource will be used by the blue whale and not by the many other species that prey on krill in the Antarctic. The latter is probably the most flawed assumption, as many other species would be able to respond more quickly to an increased resource than the blue whale.

The question of competition for resources also extends to competition with us. For example some fishermen in the North Atlantic are concerned about competition with minke whales for commercial fish species, such as herring, or that minkes are competing with commercially important species for prey. Clearly minke whales are going to be an important marine species in conservation, management and environmental change issues in the twenty-first century. We are beginning to understand the minke's place in the world's marine ecosystems, but there is still much we need to learn. In the future, we look forward to more of the type of interaction where people enjoy and appreciate the living minke whale for what it is, and for its ecological and esthetic value.

MINKE WHALES DISTRIBUTION MAP

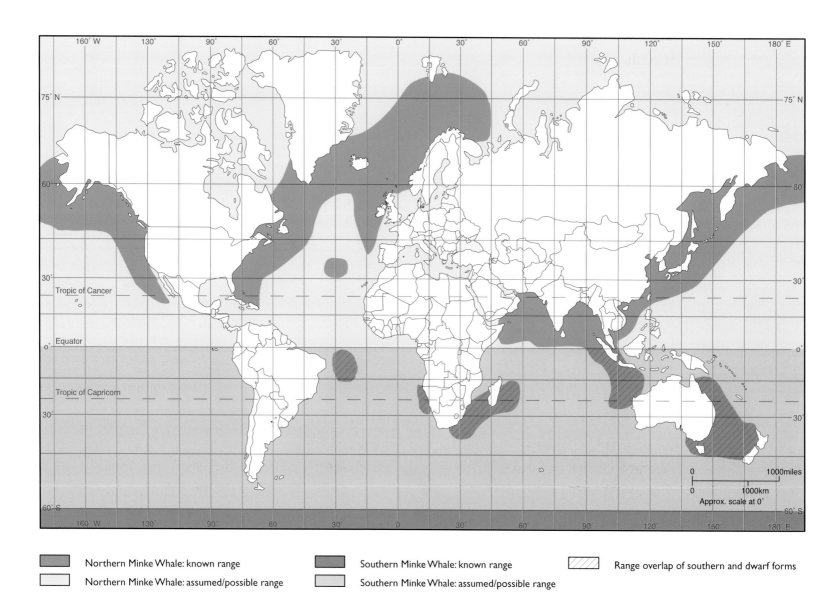

■ Northern Minke Whale: known range	■ Southern Minke Whale: known range	⧄ Range overlap of southern and dwarf forms
□ Northern Minke Whale: assumed/possible range	□ Southern Minke Whale: assumed/possible range	

Minke Whale Facts

Common name	minke whale
Scientific names	*Balaenoptera acutorostrata, B. bonaerensis* (following the recent classification by Rice, 1999).
Other names	least finner, little piked whale, pikehead, sharpheaded finner, lesser rorqual

B. acutorostrata (northern hemisphere)

	Female	Male
Maximum Adult Length	30 ft (9.1 m)	29 ft (8.8 m)
Average Length at Sexual Maturity	24 ft 4 in (7.4 m)	22½ ft (6.9 m)
Average Weight at Sexual Maturity	4–5 tonnes	4–5 tonnes
Gestation	10 months	
Age at Maturity	7–8 years	7–8 years
Longevity	up to 60 years	up to 60 years

B. bonaerensis (southern hemisphere)

	Female	Male
Maximum Adult Length	35 ft (10.7 m)	32 ft (9.8 m)
Average Length at Sexual Maturity	26 ft (7.9 m)	24½ ft (7.9 m)
Average Weight at Sexual Maturity	4–5 tonnes	4–5 tonnes
Gestation	10 months	
Age at Maturity	7–8 years	7–8 years
Longevity	up to 60 years	up to 60 years

Dwarf Minke (*B. acutorostrata* in the southern hemisphere)

Life history details are not yet known, but the maximum length is approximately 24 ft 4 in (7.4 m) for females, and 22 ft 4 in (6.8 m) for males.

Biographical Note

Rus Hoelzel earned his Ph.D in genetics in Cambridge, England and has worked at the Population Biology Centre, Imperial College, U.K., the National Cancer Institute in the U.S.A. and is presently a Reader in the Biological Sciences Department at the University of Durham in the U.K. He has studied the behavioral ecology and population genetics of marine mammals since the 1970s. Jonathan Stern earned his Ph.D at Texas A&M University, Galveston, studying spatial and temporal distribution and movement patterns of baleen whales, and currently lectures in biology there. He has worked on studying the population biology and feeding ecology of marine mammals since the 1970s.

Together with Dr Ellie Dorsey in the early 1980s, the authors were the first to apply the field observational techniques pioneered on killer whales and humpback whales to the minke whale. This work was conducted in waters off Washington State, U.S.A. and British Columbia, Canada, and later by Jonathan Stern off California.

Recommended Reading

Dorsey, E.M., Stern, S.J., Hoelzel, A.R. & Jacobsen, J., Recognition of individual minke whales from the west coast of North America, International Whale Commission Special Issue 12: 357-368, 1990.

Hoelzel, A.R., Dorsey, E.M. & Stern, S.J., The foraging specializations of individual minke whales, Animal Behaviour 38: 786-794, 1989.

Horwood, J., The biology and exploitation of minke whales, CRC Press, 1990.

Rice, D.W., Marine Mammals of the World; Systematics and Distribution, Special Publication No. 4, Society for Marine Mammalogy, 1999.

Wada, S., Genetic distinction between two minke whale stocks in the Okhotsk Sea coast of Japan, International Whale Commission. (SC/43/Mi32), 1991.

Index

*Entries in **bold** indicate pictures*